First World War
and Army of Occupation
War Diary
France, Belgium and Germany

59 DIVISION
177 Infantry Brigade
Headquarters
27 January 1915 - 29 February 1916

WO95/3022/1

Published by

The Naval & Military Press Ltd

Unit 10 Ridgewood Industrial Park,

Uckfield, East Sussex,

TN22 5QE England

Tel: +44 (0) 1825 749494

www.naval-military-press.com

www.nmarchive.com

This diary has been reprinted in facsimile from the original. Any imperfections are inevitably reproduced and the quality may fall short of modern type and cartographic standards.

© **Crown Copyright**
Images reproduced by permission of The National Archives, London, England, 2015.

Contents

Document type	Place/Title	Date From	Date To
Heading	WO95/3022/1 1915 Jan-1916 Feb 59 Division Headquarters		
Heading	59 Division HQ. 177 Bde 1915 Jan-1916 Feb		
War Diary	Luton	27/01/1915	22/02/1915
War Diary	Luton-Brentwood	25/02/1915	26/02/1915
War Diary	Brentwood	27/02/1915	10/03/1915
War Diary	Brentwood-Luton	11/03/1915	11/03/1915
War Diary	Luton	08/04/1915	02/08/1915
War Diary	Luton-St Albans	05/08/1915	05/08/1915
War Diary	St Albans	06/08/1915	20/10/1915
War Diary	St Albans-Harpenden	22/10/1915	22/10/1915
War Diary	Harpenden	26/10/1915	30/12/1915
Heading	177th (Infantry) Brigade From January 1st-1916 To January 31st 1916		
War Diary	Harpenden	05/01/1916	29/01/1916
Heading	War Diary of 177th Infy Brigade From Feb 1st 1916 to Feb 29th 1916		
War Diary	Harpenden	14/02/1916	29/02/1916

WO 1a5/3022/1

1916 Jan – 1916 Feb   5a Division
Headquarters

59 DIVISION

HQ 177 BDE

1915 JAN — 1916 FEB

Army Form C. 2118.

WAR DIARY
or
INTELLIGENCE SUMMARY.
(Erase heading not required.)

Instructions regarding War Diaries and Intelligence Summaries are contained in F. S. Regs., Part II. and the Staff Manual respectively. Title pages will be prepared in manuscript.

177 L/Hzu?

Hour, Date, Place	Summary of Events and Information	Remarks and References to Appendices
LUTON		
27. 1. 15	Brigade Major - Lieut Col R STAVELEY arrives and reports to HQ 2/1 NM Division - he takes over Offices in Carnegie (public) Library LUTON. 2/5 LINCOLNSHIRE REGT have arrived previously	
28. 1. 15	Brigade Commander Col G.M. JACKSON. TD arrived LUTON and takes over Command of the 2/1 Lincoln & Leicester Brigade & reports to 2/1 N.M.Div HQs. The 2/4 Lincolnshire Regt arrives LUTON from LINCOLN & is taken on the Strength of Brigade	
29. 1. 15	2/4 Leicestershire Regt arrives LUTON from LEICESTER and is taken on Strength of the Brigade	
30. 1. 15	2/5 Leicestershire Regt arrives LUTON from LOUGHBOROUGH and is taken on Strength of the Brigade.	
9. 2. 15	The G.O.C. 2/1 NM Div Brig Genl A.B. McCall CB inspects 2/5 Leicestershire Regt in Stockwood Park	
11. 2. 15	The G.O.C. 2/1 NM Div Brig Genl H.B. McCall CB inspects 2/4 Lincolnshire Regt in STOCKWOOD PARK	

Army Form C. 2118.

WAR DIARY
or
INTELLIGENCE SUMMARY.
(Erase heading not required.)

Hour, Date, Place	Summary of Events and Information	Remarks and References to Appendices
LUTON. 22-2-15	Jahanesle Rifles arrive	
	Inspection of 2/1 MM Div by Lieut Genl SIR IAN HAMILTON KCB in LUTON HOO PARK	
LUTON - BRENTWOOD 25-2-15	Brigade HQ moved to BRENTWOOD for Trench digging	
	2/4 Lincolnshire Regt to Billets in Ongar	
	2/5 " " " " in Billericay	
	The day previous 24-2-15	
	2/4 Leicestershire Regt to Billets in HODDESDON	
	2/5 " " " " EPPING	
26-2-15	1/1 Lincoln &Leicester Brigade lecture England to join BEF in France	
BRENTWOOD 27-2-15	Capt HS HASSALL 1/5 Lincolnshire Regt 2nd Brigade as Staff Captain Confirmed in LONDON GAZETTE 28-4-15- antedate to 27.2.15-	

Army Form C. 2118.

WAR DIARY
or
INTELLIGENCE SUMMARY.
(Erase heading not required.)

Instructions regarding War Diaries and Intelligence
Summaries are contained in F. S. Regs., Part II.
and the Staff Manual respectively. Title pages
will be prepared in manuscript.

Hour, Date, Place	Summary of Events and Information	Remarks and references to Appendices
BRENTWOOD		
10 - 3 - 15	2/5 Leicestershire Regt moves back from billets in EPPING	
BRENTWOOD—LUTON	to billets in LUTON.	
11 - 3 - 15	Brigade HQ return to Carnegie Library LUTON	
	2/4 Lincolnshire Regt move from billets ONGAR to billets LUTON	
	2/5 " " " " " " " LUTON	
	2/4 Leicestershire Regt " " " " HUDDESDON " " LUTON	
LUTON		
8 - 4 - 15	Lieut C/F SHIELDS 2/5 Leicestershire Regt proceeds to BEF	
11 - 4 - 15	Maj Genl Sir A CODRINGTON Commanding 3rd Army	
	Personally inspects Books of { 2/4 Leicestershire Regt	
	{ 2/5 Leicestershire Regt	
14 - 4 - 15	Maj Genl Sir A CODRINGTON { 2/4 Lincolns	
	Personally inspect Books { 2/5 Lincolns	
30 - 4 - 15	Lieut W.A. FOX 2/4 Lincolns proceeds overseas to join	(killed in action 26/7/15)
	1st Line Unit	

WAR DIARY or INTELLIGENCE SUMMARY

Army Form C. 2118.

(Erase heading not required.)

Instructions regarding War Diaries and Intelligence Summaries are contained in F.S. Regs., Part II. and the Staff Manual respectively. Title pages will be prepared in manuscript.

Hour, Date, Place	Summary of Events and Information	Remarks and References to Appendices
LUTON		
10-5-15	2nd Lieuts E.F.PRICE & J.R.LEESON 2/4 Quarters to BEF overseas	
15-5-15	2nd Lieut L.H.PEARSON 2/5 decorates proceeds overseas to BEF	
18-6-15	Home Service men separated from their Units and transferred to Provisional Battn SOUTHEND	
	2/4 Lincolnshire Regt 3 Officers 297 Rank & file	
	2/5 " " " 1 " 319 " "	
	2/4 Leicestershire Regt 3 " 203 " "	
	2/5 " " 0 " 183 " "	
20-6-15	2/4 Lincolns Send 40 men Overseas to join 1st Line Unit	
	2/4 Leicesters " 129 " " " " " " "	
	2/5 Leicesters " 132 " " " " " " "	
7-7-15	Officers 2/5 Leicesters proceed overseas to join BEF	
	2nd Lts R.C.LAWTON - E.E.WYNNE. N.C.MARRIOT. C.B.WILLIAMS and C.L.SAUNDERS	

WAR DIARY
or
INTELLIGENCE SUMMARY.
(Erase heading not required.)

Army Form C. 2118.

Hour, Date, Place	Summary of Events and Information	Remarks and References to Appendices
LUTON.		
13-7-15	Following Officers proceed overseas to join B.E.F.	
	2/4 Lincolns hire Regt	
	Lieut MAPLES. 2nd Lieuts ELLIS-CLIXBY. CHANCELLOR.	
	2/4 Leicestershire Regt	
	Lieut WHITTINGHAM	
	W.R.SCHOLES- B.E.W.MUGRIDGE G.D.ADAMS.	
	C.F.WRIGHT F.C.BLUNT F.N.WALTERS	
16-7-15	Brigade moves under Canvas in Stockwood-Park (LUTON)	
21-7-15	2nd Lieut SHERWELL 2/4 Lincolns proceeds overseas to join 1st Line Unit.	
2-8-7	Following Officers proceed overseas to B.E.F	
	2/4 Lincolns 2nd Lieuts BRUNWIN-HALES and WOOD	
	2/4 Leicesters Lieut ABELL 2/Lieut F.PAPPERELL	

Army Form C. 2118.

WAR DIARY
or
INTELLIGENCE SUMMARY.
(Erase heading not required.)

Hour, Date, Place	Summary of Events and Information	Remarks and References to Appendices
LUTON – ST ALBANS 5-8-15	Brigade less 2/4 Lincolns & 2/4 Leicesters moves Camp from STOCKWOOD PARK (LUTON) to BRITONS CAMP (ST ALBANS)	
ST ALBANS 6 8-15	2/4 Lincolns & 2/4 Leicesters arrive in BRITONS CAMP from STOCKWOOD PARK CAMP (LUTON)	
10-5-15	Brigade Training begins	
13-8-15	Numerals Adopted 2/1 Lincoln 4 Leicester Bde becomes 177th Bde of 59th W. M. Div.	CRS
15 8-15 / 16 8-15	2/4 Lincolns send Instr 134 NCOs & men overseas to BEF 2/5 Leicester Send 116 NCOs & men overseas to BEF	
23 8 15	2/5 Leicester officers Lieut J.H. HASS 2nd Lts C.B. CLAY CRS NC STONEHAM posted overseas to BEF	
18 8-15	2/4 Lincolns send Capt S PILKINGTON. Capt AR FORSELL Lieut NC HOBBS. 2nd Lieuts QE RUSSELL. CH WAGSTAFF overseas to join BEF	

WAR DIARY
or
INTELLIGENCE SUMMARY.
(Erase heading not required.)

Army Form C. 2118.

Hour, Date, Place	Summary of Events and Information	Remarks and References to Appendices
ST. ALBANS		
19. 9. 15	2/4 Lincolns Send draft of 100 men to B.E.F.	
21. 9. 15	Zeppelin Guard mounted (first night) Divisional Operations in vicinity of RODDESDEN PARK near HEMEL-HEMPSTEAD	
22. 9. 15	Brigade returns to Camp - by units arriving between 10-30 & 11-45 pm.	
1. 10. 15	Inspection of 59th N.M.Dn on GORHAMBURY PARK by Lt. Genl Sir L Rundle KCB.	
6. 10. 15	2/4 Lincolns send 2/Lt HORNE to B.E.F	
8. 10. 15	Instructs is due received for reducing Strength of all units to 600. Surplus to be transferred to 3rd Line units or Provisional Battn. at Brighton SOUTHEND. according to age & fitness	

WAR DIARY
or
INTELLIGENCE SUMMARY.
(Erase heading not required.)

Army Form C. 2118.

Hour, Date, Place	Summary of Events and Information	Remarks and References to Appendices
ST. ALBANS 18-10-15	Divisional Operations (convoy) & Aeroplane attached to each side for observation — Our Aeroplane (White Face) fails in attempting to land at White Face H.Q. Observer very severely injured — Pilot slightly. 9.30 pm Zeppelin passes over BRITONS CAMP toward LONDON from direction of HATFIELD, N. Promptly evacuated — Troops bivouac into surrounding fields & under fences. Bayard Operations.	
20-10-15 ST. ALBANS – HARPENDEN 22-10-15 HARPENDEN	Brigade less 2/5-Lincolns from Stoke Camp and mine into Billets in HARPENDEN	
26-10-15	2/4 Lincolns and 2d/5 H.R. POCHIN. L.F.H.W. de SZAHHMOWIEZ BTC. GILBERT & LC: BARTON to BEF	

WAR DIARY
INTELLIGENCE SUMMARY

Army Form C. 2118.

Hour, Date, Place	Summary of Events and Information	Remarks and References to Appendices
HARPENDEN		
9·9 10-15	2/5 Lincolns arrive from BRITONS CAMP ST ALBANS and go into Billets. HARPENDEN.	
	2/5 Leicesters send Nerveos to B.E.F. Capt S.J.FOWLER 2dLt J.R.BROOKS. H.W.OLIVER A.L.MACBETH. C.H.PICKWORTH	
3 11-15	Divisional Operations around HILLEND.Fm	
5- 11-15	2nd Lieut C SELWYN 2/5-Leicesters to B.E.F.	
7- 11-15	At 9.0m Civil Police warn Bg HQ that Zeppelin is in SAFFRON WALDRON district. All precautions taken - Emergency (by 2/5 Lincolns) turns out at 10-15 it returns to Billets having heard nor seen See or heard of any Aircraft	Cns
9- 11- 15-	Inspection of 2/4 & 2/5 Lincolns by Maj Genl DIXON Inspector General of Infantry (a long wet morning)	

Army Form C. 2118.

WAR DIARY
or
INTELLIGENCE SUMMARY.
(Erase heading not required.)

Instructions regarding War Diaries and Intelligence Summaries are contained in F. S. Regs., Part II. and the Staff Manual respectively. Title pages will be prepared in manuscript.

Hour, Date, Place	Summary of Events and Information	Remarks and References to Appendices
HARPENDEN		
14-11-15	Maj Genl R M F READ - C B Takes over Command of 59th N M Div from Brig Genl H B McCALL CB	
17-11-15	GOC inspects Brigade in ROTHAMSTED PARK after inspection Bde proceeds on Rout March & defile past GOC - on 2nd homeward march - (Very funty) Horses & Transport were sent to Stables after inspection. 2nd Lieut S F LENNARD 2/4 deseates to BEF	
19-11-15	Japanese Rifles withdrawn from all units and .303 Substituted, these are old & unsuitable for musketry Practices.	
24-11-15	The GOC witnesses Bombers trained by Lieut PICKIN 2/4 decorates they also see Tench (Catapult) explode mine, charge & Bomb at trenches	

Army Form C. 2118.

WAR DIARY
or
INTELLIGENCE SUMMARY.
(Erase heading not required.)

Instructions regarding War Diaries and Intelligence Summaries are contained in F.S. Regs., Part II. and the Staff Manual respectively. Title pages will be prepared in manuscript.

Hour, Date, Place	Summary of Events and Information	Remarks and References to Appendices
HARPENDEN		
26-11-15	Divisional (Road) Operation on WATLING STREET NE of REDBOURNE	
29-11-15	Two Companies of each Unit Commence a 3 weeks Course of Special Training	
2-12-15	Brigade Operation + 1 Bat RFA + 1 Bat Hows + Div Cyclist Coy + Harrow School OTC (350) + St Albans School OTC (80) - in SANDRIDGE - HILLEND FARM District. G.O.C. attends and after Conclusion inspects School Corps	Cas
4-12-15	G.O.C. holds Officers in their Messes in the afternoon.	
6-12-15	Buffalo take over (2/6 Leicesters) from 176th Brigade the Aerial Observation post at HAMMONDS FARM	

Form C. 2118/10.
(9 29 6) W 3332—1107 103,000 10/13 H W V

Army Form C. 2118.

WAR DIARY
or
INTELLIGENCE SUMMARY.
(Erase heading not required.)

Instructions regarding War Diaries and Intelligence Summaries are contained in F. S. Regs., Part II. and the Staff Manual respectively. Title pages will be prepared in manuscript.

Hour, Date, Place	Summary of Events and Information	Remarks and References to Appendices
HARPENDEN		
12-12-15	Snowing heavy. Snow storm about 9 a.m. Maurice Farman Biplane No 6688. Pilot Lieut A P Dickie RFC alighted 500y+ E of HARPENDEN - G.N. Railway Station. Guard mounted over it 1st by 2/4 Lincolns relieved at 11 a.m. by 2/5 Leicesters relieved at 5-30 p.m. by 2/5 Lincolns. Lieut Dickie decided to remain the night.	CRS
13-12-15	Lieut A P Dickie RFC in (MF) Biplane No 6688 rose at 11-15 a.m. bound for CATTERICK (YORKS)	
15-12-15	Brigade Route march of the 2 Special Training Companies of Brigade distance estimated 9 ½ miles. Weather Bad - Snowing all day. Time 8 a.m. to 4-40 p.m. - Dinners from Field Kitchens. Strength - Officers 28 - Rank & file 1153. Casualties Nil.	

Form A. 2118/10.

WAR DIARY
or
INTELLIGENCE SUMMARY.
(Erase heading not required.)

Army Form C. 2118.

Hour, Date, Place	Summary of Events and Information	Remarks and References to Appendices
HARPENDEN 18 -12 -15	Divi Conference of Each Unit Complete 2 weeks Special Training Course	
92. 12 - 15	Divisional Operations 59th Div concentrating on HENDON - in 3 Columns from present billet areas. 177th Bde is No 3 Column Div Cyclist Coy covering left flank after reaching St ALBANS.	CRO
98 ~~29~~ 12 - 15	G.O.C. 59th Div with 7 other Divisional Brigade Staff Officers proceed on a 6 days Tour Overseas	
30 12 - 15	Brigade Route March 12 Miles - 7hours. 9 to 5 p.m.	

Confidential

War Diary.

of

177th (Infantry) Brigade

From Jany 1st 1916   to Jany 31st 1916

C R Staveley Lt Col
Bde Major
for G.O.C. 177th Bde

177th Infty Brigade WAR DIARY
INTELLIGENCE SUMMARY
(Erase heading not required.)

Army Form C. 2118.

Instructions regarding War Diaries and Intelligence Summaries are contained in F. S. Regs., Part II. and the Staff Manual respectively. Title pages will be prepared in manuscript.

HEADQUARTERS 8 - FEB 1916 177th INFANTRY BRIGADE No. S/10/

Hour, Date, Place	Summary of Events and Information	Remarks and references to Appendices
1916 HARPENDEN 5-1-16	Brigadier Genl C.R. BLACKADER. DSO takes over Command of 177th Bde from Col Brigade Commandr Q.M. JACKSON	CRS
6.1.16	2 Companies of each Unit Commence a 3½ weeks Course of "Special Training"	CRS
18.1.16	Machine Gun Sections of all 4 Units with Horses Limber wagons and all present Equipment — Inspected by M.G.O. 59th Me Div at ST ALBANS 11-30 am	CRS
22.1.16	Units (less 2/6 Lincolns) receive their 2nd-drafts of ("DERBY") Recruits - Towards (raising Strengths to 850 Rank & File	CRS
29.1.16	2 Companies f each Unit Complete 3½ weeks Special Training Course	CRS
" " "	Undermentioned Units Complete receipt f ("Derby") Recruits to bring each up to 850 Rank & File	CRS
	2/4 Lincolns during receive d Since 22/1/16 269 Recruits	
	2/4 Leicesters " " " " 287 "	
	2/5 Leicesters " " " " 170 "	

Confidential

War Diary
of
177th Infy Brigade

From Feb 1st 1916 to Feb 29th 1916

177th Infy Brigade

WAR DIARY
INTELLIGENCE SUMMARY.
(Erase heading not required.)

Army Form C. 2118.

Hour, Date, Place	Summary of Events and Information	Remarks and references to Appendices
HARPENDEN. 14-2-16	Maj Genl A E Sandbach C.B. DSO R.E. takes over Command of 59th (N.M.) Divn from Maj Genl R.N.R. Reade CB.	Cpy
" "	2/5 Lincolnshire Regt complete receipt of Recruits to bring Strength up to 850 Rank & File. From Jany 29th to 14th Feby inclusive total received 334. These are (Volunteer) Recruits. Coys 2, 3, 4, 5 (Unnamed) D.S.P.	Cpy
17.2.16	Major G.B.G. Wood Denbenshire Fusiliers takes over from Lt Col C.R. Staveley — duties of Brigade Major of 177th Bde	Cpd
24.2.16	Maj Gen. A E SANDBACH CB DSO inspected the Recruits of 2/4th & 2/5th LINCOLNSHIRE Regt & 2/5th LEICESTERSHIRE Regt. & the Quarantine of the 2/4th	Cpn
		approved Maj Gen C/ Brigade Maj 14 for Bde Cmdr 177th Infy Brigade

177th Infy Brigade.

Army Form C. 2118.

WAR DIARY
or
INTELLIGENCE SUMMARY.
(Erase heading not required.)

Instructions regarding War Diaries and Intelligence Summaries are contained in F. S. Regs., Part II. and the Staff Manual respectively. Title pages will be prepared in manuscript.

Hour, Date, Place	Summary of Events and Information	Remarks and references to Appendices
HARTENDEN 23.2.16	2 Lewis Guns received for the Brigade. Each Batt. now has one gun. W.E. Part VIII much affected by the storms.	GM GM
29.2.16	Test mine Emergency schemes "B" carried out.	GM

M.W. Ward Major
O/C 2/5 Royal Hussars
Regt 2/5th
for Brig. General Commander
177th Infy Brigade

www.ingramcontent.com/pod-product-compliance
Lightning Source LLC
Chambersburg PA
CBHW081508160426

43193CB00014B/2624